To Ruth —

— From Don.

On a day of loveliness,   — Easter 1935. —
Made twice lovely,
By her love . . . .

UNPUBLISHED EARLY POEMS

THE MACMILLAN COMPANY
NEW YORK · BOSTON · CHICAGO · DALLAS
ATLANTA · SAN FRANCISCO

MACMILLAN & CO., LIMITED
LONDON · BOMBAY · CALCUTTA
MELBOURNE

THE MACMILLAN COMPANY
OF CANADA, LIMITED
TORONTO

UNPUBLISHED EARLY POEMS

BY ALFRED TENNYSON

EDITED BY CHARLES TENNYSON

HIS GRANDSON

NEW YORK

THE MACMILLAN COMPANY

1932

Copyright, 1932
By THE MACMILLAN COMPANY

All rights reserved — no part of this book may be reproduced in any form without permission in writing from the publisher, except by a reviewer who wishes to quote brief passages in connection with a review written for inclusion in magazine or newspaper.

Printed and Published, February, 1932.

Printed in the United States of America.

PREFACE

THE poems contained in this volume were never published by Tennyson, or, with one exception to which I will refer later, by his son, Hallam Lord Tennyson, in whose possession the MS. of them remained until his death in 1928. He left them, with other MSS., to me with liberty to publish at my discretion.

The great majority of the poems date from the poet's boyhood and his residence at Cambridge, and I have divided the material into three sections, headed respectively "Boyhood," "Cambridge Period," and "1830–1842."

The first two sections are very much the most important, and in these I have included one poem ("The Coach of Death") which was published by Hallam Tennyson in his Memoir of the poet, in order to gather into one volume all the very remarkable Juvenilia which are not to be found in the authorised editions of Tennyson's works.

"The Devil and the Lady," which was issued by Messrs. Macmillan in February 1930, gave the world convincing evidence of Tennyson's the "Lotos-Eaters," "Oenone," "Ulysses," and "Tithonus."

So, too, with the Blank Verse. This has passed from the Shakespearean exercise of "The Devil and the Lady," through the Miltonics of "Armageddon" to a freer and richer style (which, however, still shows traces of Milton and Shakespeare) in the lines "Working High Treason." These lead up to the "Lover's Tale," which was written in 1831–32, and represent a further stage in the evolution of a verse flexible and rich enough to achieve "Oenone," "The Gardener's Daughter," and the "Morte D'Arthur." A similar development, though along a line which Tennyson never carried further, is that from the rhymed couplets of the Proserpine fragment to those which begin and end the "Vision of Sin," published twenty years later. In these twenty years the couplet has passed from the mechanical brilliance and regularity characteristic of the eighteenth century to a freedom and trochaic lightness which make it almost unrecognisable. These are the only two examples of rhymed heroic verse in Tennyson's published work, though there exists in MS. in the Library of Trinity College, Cambridge, a poem in this metre, on the retreat of Napoleon from Moscow, which seems to represent an intermediate style. There are, unfortunately, no traces of any early experiments leading up to the wonderful Spenserian stanzas of the "Lotos-Eaters," Tennyson's only extant attempt at that historic form. It is remarkable, having regard to his early admiration for Spenser, Thomson and Byron, that no trace of an apprenticeship to Spenser's great stanza survives.

Mention may also be made of the collection of sonnets, all but one apparently written in the poet's nineteenth and twentieth years. Tennyson is commonly held to have failed in this form. Many of these sonnets, though imperfect in finish, seem to me superior to most of those in the published works and suggest that, had the poet cared to persevere with this form of composition, he would have become a master of the art. The number of different rhyme schemes employed is remarkable. Of the ten sonnets printed only two have similar arrangements; only one is on the true Italian model; one normal Shakespearean, and the remainder all more or less irregular.

Something should perhaps be said of the poems entitled "Marion," "Lisette," and "Amy," which recall "Lilian," "Rosalind," "Eleanore," etc., in the volumes of 1830 and 1832. These early poems have been adversely criticised, often with little discrimination. They are the work of a

Parts of the "Rape of Proserpine" and "Armageddon" and all the other poems included in the volume, with the exception of "The Coach of Death," "In Deep and Solemn Dreams," "Sense and Conscience" and "The Outcast," appeared in *The Nineteenth Century and After* (issues for March, April and May 1931).

I am indebted to the Trustees of the late Hallam Lord Tennyson for permission to include "The Coach of Death."

C. T.

CONTENTS

PART I. BOYHOOD.
	PAGE
Translation from Claudian's "Proserpine"	1
Armageddon	6
The Coach of Death	17
Ode: O Bosky Brook	23
The Outcast	28
In Deep and Solemn Dreams	30
Memory	33
Perdidi Diem	35

PART II. CAMBRIDGE.
Playfellow Winds	41
Sense and Conscience	42
"Ilion, Ilion"	47
Elegiacs	49
Marion	50
Lisette	52
Amy	54
Lines to the picture of a young lady of Fashion	56

Sonnets:

She took the dappled partridge	58
Alas! how weary	59
Hail, Light	60
The Wise, the Pure	61
Woe to the double-tongued	62
Ah, fade not yet	63
I lingered yet awhile	64

Sonnets (*continued*) PAGE
    When that rank heat 65
    Conrad! why call thy life . . . 66
Milton's Mulberry 67

PART III. 1830–1842.
    The ruined kiln 71
    Fragment: Over the dark world . . . 72
    Britain 73
    What Thor said to the Bard 75
    Sonnet: How thought you 77
    New Year's Eve 78
    An Idle Rhyme 79
APPENDIX 81

PART I
BOYHOOD

TRANSLATION FROM CLAUDIAN'S
"PROSERPINE"

T H E gloomy chariot of the God of night,
And the wan stars that sicken'd at the sight,
And the dark nuptials of th' infernal King,
With senses rapt in holy thought, I sing.
Away! away! profane ones! ye whose days
Are spent in endless sin and error's maze,
Seraphic transports through my bosom roll,
All Phoebus fills my heart and fires my soul.
Lo! the shrines tremble and a heavenly light
Streams from their vaulted roofs serenely bright,
The God! the God, appears! the yawning ground
Moans at the view, the temples quake around,
And high in air the Eleusinians raise
The sacred torch with undulating blaze;
Hiss the green snakes to sacred rapture giv'n
And meekly lift their scaly necks to heav'n,
With easy lapse they win their gentle way
And rear their rosy crests and listen to my lay.
See! see! where triform Hecate dimly stands,
And mild Iacchus leads the tuneful bands!
Immortal glories round his temples shine,
And flow'ring ivy wreaths his brows entwine;
From Parthia's land he clasps beneath his chin
The speckled honours of the tiger's skin;
A vine-clad thyrsus with celestial grace
Sustains his reeling feet and props his falling pace.

Ye mighty demons, whose tremendous sway
The shadowy tribes of airy ghosts obey,
To whose insatiate portion ever fall
All things that perish on this earthly ball,
Whom livid Styx with lurid torrent bounds
And fiery Phlegethon for aye surrounds,
Dark, deep and whirling round his flaming caves
The braying vortex of his breathless waves,
Eternal spirits! to your bard explain
The dread Arcana of the Stygian reign,
How that stern Deity, Infernal Jove,
First felt the power, and own'd the force of love;
How Hell's fair Empress first was snatch'd away
From Earth's bright regions, and the face of day;
How anxious Ceres wander'd far and near
Now torn by grief and tortur'd now by fear,
Whence laws to man are giv'n, and acorns yield
To the rich produce of the golden field.
Hell's haughty Lord in times of old began
To rouse 'gainst Heav'n the terrors of his clan;
Stern fury shook his soul—that he alone
Of every God upon his glitt'ring throne,
Should lead a dull and melancholy life,
Without the fond endearments of a wife—
Wretch that he was, who knew not how to claim
A consort's or a father's dearer name!
Now Hell's misshapen monsters rush to arms
And fill the wide abyss with loud alarms;
The haggard train of midnight Furies meet
To shake the Thunderer from his starry seat,
And pale Tisiphone, with baleful breath
Calls the thin Ghosts within the camp of Death;

High in her hand amid the shades of night
The gleaming pine shoots forth a dismal light,
Around her head the snaky volumes rise
And dart their tongues of flame and roll their gory eyes.
Now had all nature gone to wrack again
And Earth's fell offspring burst their brazen chain,
And from the deep recesses where they lay
Uprisen in wrath to view the beam of day,
Now had the fierce Aegaeon thrown aside
The adamantine limits of his pride,
Uprear'd his hundred-handed form on high
And dar'd the forkéd terrors of the sky;
But the dire Parcae with a piercing yell
Before the throne of gloomy Pluto fell,
Around his knees their suppliant hands were thrown,
Those awful hands which make the world their own,
Whose dreadful power the shades of Hades fear
And men on earth, and Gods in Heav'n revere,
Which mark the lot of fate's unerring page
And ply their iron tasks through every age.
First Lachesis began (while all around
Hell's hollow caverns shudder'd at the sound),
"Dark Power of night and God of Hell, for whom
We draw the fated threads of human doom,
Thou end and origin of all on earth,
Redeeming death below by human birth!
Thou Lord of life and dissolution! King
Of all that live! (for first from thee they spring
And to thee they return, and in thy reign
Take other shapes and seek the world again)
Break not, ah! break not with unholy deed
That peace our laws have fix'd, our threats decreed.

3

Oh, wake not thou the trumpet's impious swell
Nor raise thy standard in the gulph of Hell
Nor rouse the Titans from their dread abode,
The hideous Titans, foes to man and God.
Jove,—Jove himself shall grant thine ardent wish
And some fond wife shall crown thy nuptial bliss."
She spake—the God was struck with sudden shame
And his wild fury lost its former flame.
So when with whirlwinds in his icy train
Stern Boreas sweeps along the sounding plain,
Bright o'er his wings the glittering frost is spread
And deathless winters crown his hoary head,
Then bow the groves, the woods his breath obey,
The heaving Ocean tosses either way.
But lo! if chance on far Aeolia's shores
The God of winds should close his brazen doors,
With sudden pause the jarring tumults cease,
And Earth, Air, Ocean, find one common peace.
Then Maia's son he calls, in haste to bear
His fix'd commands through all the deep of air;
Prompt at the word Cyllenius is at hand
Adorn'd with pinion'd brow and magic wand.
Himself the God of terrors, rear'd on high,
Sits thron'd in shades of midnight majesty,
Dim wreaths of mist his mighty sceptre shroud,
He veils his horrors in a viewless cloud.
Then thus in haughty tone the God began
(Through Hell's wide halls the echoing accents ran,
The bellowing beast that guards the gates of Hell
Repress'd the thunder of his triple yell,
And sad Cocytus at the sudden cry
Recall'd his wailing stream of misery.

From Acheron's banks no sullen murmurs spread,
His hoarse waves slumbered on his noiseless bed,
'Gan Phlegethon in surly haste retire
And still his whirling waves and check his flood of fire),
"Grandson of Atlas, thou whose footsteps stray
Through Hell's deep shadows, and the realms of day,
To whom alone of all the Gods 'tis giv'n
To tread the shores of Styx and halls of Heav'n,
Chain of each world and link of either sphere,
Whom Tegea's sons in silent awe revere,
Go, cleave the winds and bear my will to Jove,
That haughty God who sways the realms above. . . .

Note.—This is a free translation into 133 English lines of the first 93 lines of Claudian's "De Raptu Proserpinae."

The MS. of this fragment is in the same notebook as that of the earliest version of "The Devil and the Lady," which it precedes. The title-page of the notebook is inscribed "Translation of Claudian's Proserpine, by A. Tennyson," and bears no reference to "The Devil and the Lady," so that the Claudian translation is evidently the earlier poem of the two, and the earliest extant poem by Tennyson. He himself said that he wrote "hundreds and hundreds of lines in the regular Popeian metre," after reading Pope's "Iliad," which was a favourite book of his when he was about eleven or twelve.

The first draft of "The Devil and the Lady" was written when he was fourteen (see the Preface to the edition published by Macmillan & Co. in February 1930), and this translation, therefore, belongs to a period between the eleventh and fourteenth years of the poet.

The Latin text of Claudian's lines is included in an appendix to this volume.

There was a mingling too of such strange sounds
(Which came at times upon my startled hearing)
Half wailing and half laughter ; such a dissonance
Of jarring confus'd voices, part of which
Seem'd hellish and part heavenly, whisperings,
Low chauntings, strangled screams, and other notes
Which I may liken unto nothing which
I ever heard on Earth, but seem'd most like
A mixture of the voice of man and beast;
And then again throughout the lurid waste
Of air, a breathless stillness reigned, so deep,
So deathlike, so appalling, that I shrunk
Into myself again, and almost wish'd
For the recurrence of those deadly sounds,
Which fix'd my senses into stone, and drove
The buoyant life-drops back into my heart.

Nor did the glittering of white wings escape
My notice far within the East, which caught
Ruddy reflection from the ensanguin'd West;
Nor, ever and anon, the shrill clear sound
Of some aerial trumpet, solemnly
Pealing throughout the Empyrean void.

Thus to some wakeful hind who on the heights
Outwatches the wan planet, comes the sound
Of some far horn along the distant hills
Echoing, in some beleaguer'd country, where
The pitiless Enemy by night hath made
Sudden incursion and unsafe inroad.

The streams, whose imperceptible advance
Lingering in slow meanders, once was wont

To fertilize the plain beneath—whose course
Was barely mark'd save by the lazy straws
That wandered down them—now, as instinct with life,
Ran like the lightning's wing, and dash'd upon
The curvature of their green banks a wreath
Of lengthen'd foam; and yet, although they rush'd
Incalculably swift and fring'd with spray
The pointed crags, whose wave-worn slippery height
Parted their glassy channels, there awoke
No murmurs round them—but their sapphire depths
Of light were changed to crimson, as the sky
Glow'd like a fiery furnace.
                            In the East
Broad rose the moon, first like a beacon flame
Seen on the far horizon's utmost verge,
Or red eruption from the fissur'd cone
Of Cotopaxi's cloud-cap't altitude;
Then with dilated orb and mark'd with lines
Of mazy red athwart her shadowy face,
Sickly, as though her secret eyes beheld
Witchcrafts, abominations, and the spells
Of sorcerers, what time they summon up
From out the stilly chambers of the earth
Obscene, inutterable phantasies.

  The sun went down; the hot and feverish night
Succeeded; but the parch'd, unwholesome air
Was unrecruited by the tears of heaven.
There was a windless calm, a dismal pause,
A dreary interval, wherein I held
My breath and heard the beatings of my heart.
The moon show'd clearer yet, with deadlier gleam,

Her ridgéd and uneven surface stain'd
With crosses, fiery streaks, and wandering lines—
Bloody impressions! and a star or two
Peer'd through the thick and smoky atmosphere.

   Strange was that lunar light: the rock which stood
Fronting her sanguine ray, seem'd chang'd unto
A pillar of crimson, while the other half
Averted, and whatever else around
Stood not in opposition to her beams,
Was shrouded in the densest pall of night
And darkness almost palpable.
                          Deep fear
And trembling came upon me, when I saw
In the remotest chambers of the East
Ranges of silver tents beside the moon,
Clear, but at distance so ineffable,
That save when keenly view'd, they else might seem
But little shining points or galaxies,
The blending of the beams of many stars.

   Full opposite within the lurid West,
In clear relief against the long rich vein
Of melancholy red that fring'd the sky,
A suite of dark pavilions met mine eyes,
That covered half the western tide of Heaven,
Far stretching, in the midst of which tower'd one
Pre-eminent, which bore aloft in air
A standard, round whose staff a mighty snake
Twin'd his black folds, the while his ardent crest
And glossy neck were swaying to and fro.

II

The rustling of white wings! The bright descent
Of a young seraph! and he stood beside me
In the wide foldings of his argent robes
There on the ridge, and look'd into my face
With his unutterable shining eyes,
So that with hasty motion I did veil
My vision with both hands, and saw before me
Such coloured spots as dance before the eyes
Of those that gaze upon the noonday sun.

"O Son of Man, why stand you here alone
Upon the mountain, knowing not the things
Which will be, and the gathering of the nations
Unto the mighty battle of the Lord?
Thy sense is clogg'd with dull Mortality,
Thy spirit fetter'd with the bond of clay—
Open thine eyes and see!"
                          I look'd, but not
Upon his face, for it was wonderful
With its exceeding brightness, and the light
Of the great Angel Mind that look'd from out
The starry glowing of his restless eyes.
I felt my soul grow godlike, and my spirit
With supernatural excitation bound
Within me, and my mental eye grew large
With such a vast circumference of thought,
That, in my vanity, I seem'd to stand
Upon the outward verge and bound alone
Of God's omniscience. Each failing sense,
As with a momentary flash of light,

Grew thrillingly distinct and keen. I saw
The smallest grain that dappled the dark Earth,
The indistinctest atom in deep air,
The Moon's white cities, and the opal width
Of her small, glowing lakes, her silver heights
Unvisited with dew of vagrant cloud,
And the unsounded, undescended depth
Of her black hollows. Nay—the hum of men
Or other things talking in unknown tongues,
And notes of busy Life in distant worlds,
Beat, like a far wave, on my anxious ear.

  I wondered with deep wonder at myself:
My mind seem'd wing'd with knowledge and the
    strength
Of holy musings and immense Ideas,
Even to Infinitude. All sense of Time
And Being and Place was swallowed up and lost
Within a victory of boundless thought.
I was a part of the Unchangeable,
A scintillation of Eternal Mind,
Remix'd and burning with its parent fire.
Yea! in that hour I could have fallen down
Before my own strong soul and worshipp'd it.

  Highly and holily the Angel look'd.
Immeasurable Solicitude and Awe,
And solemn Adoration and high Faith,
Were trac'd on his imperishable front—
Then with a mournful and ineffable smile,
Which but to look on for a moment fill'd
My eyes with irresistible sweet tears,

In accents of majestic melody,
Like a swollen river's gushings in still night
Mingled with floating music, thus he spoke.

III

"O Everlasting God, and thou not less
The Everlasting Man (since that great spirit
Which permeates and informs thine inward sense,
Though limited in action, capable
Of the extreme of knowledge—whether join'd
Unto thee in conception or confin'd
From former wanderings in other shapes
I know not—deathless as its God's own life,
Burns on with inextinguishable strength),
O Lords of Earth and Tyrannies of Hell,
And thrones of Heaven, whose triple pride shall clash
In the annihilating anarchy
Of unimaginable war, a day
Of darkness riseth on ye, a thick day,
Pall'd with dun wreaths of dusky fight, a day
Of many thunders and confuséd noise,
Of bloody grapplings in the interval
Of the opposéd Battle, a great day
Of wonderful revealings and vast sights
And inconceivable visions, such as yet
Have never shone into the heart of Man—
THE DAY of the Lord God!"
        His voice grew deep
With volumes of strong sound, which made the rock
To throb beneath me, and his parted locks
Of spiral light fell raylike, as he mov'd,

On each white shoulder: his ambrosial lip
Was beautifully curv'd, as in the pride
And power of his mid Prophecy: his nostril
Dilated with Expression; half upturn'd
The broad beneficence of his clear brow
Into the smoky sky; his sunlike eyes
With tenfold glory lit; his mighty arm
Outstretch'd described half-circles; small thin flashes
Of intense lustre followed it.

IV

     I look'd,
And lo! the vision of the night was chang'd.
The sooty mantle of infernal smoke
Whose blank, obliterating, dewless cloud
Had made the plain like some vast crater, rose
Distinct from Earth and gather'd to itself
In one dense, dry, interminable mass
Sailing far Northward, as it were the shadow
Of this round Planet cast upon the face
Of the bleak air. But this was wonderful,
To see how full it was of living things,
Strange shapings, and anomalies of Hell,
And dusky faces, and protruded arms
Of hairy strength, and white and garish eyes,
And silent intertwisted thunderbolts,
Wreathing and sparkling restlessly like snakes
Within their grassy depths. I watch'd it till
Its latest margin sank beneath the sweep
Of the horizon.

     All the crimson streaks
And bloody dapplings faded from the disk
Of the immaculate morn.
        An icy veil
Of pale, weak, lifeless, thin, unnatural blue
Wrapt up the rich varieties of things
In grim and ghastly sameness.
          The clear stars
Shone out with keen but fix'd intensity,
All-silence, looking steadfast consciousness
Upon the dark and windy waste of Earth.
There was a beating in the atmosphere,
An indefinable pulsation
Inaudible to outward sense, but felt
Thro' the deep heart of every living thing,
As if the great soul of the Universe
Heav'd with tumultuous throbbings on the vast
Suspense of some grand issue. . . .

Note.—When Tennyson was in his second year at Cambridge, his father pressed him to enter for the Prize Poem (the "Chancellor's Medal"). He consented, though much against his will. The subject of the competition was "Timbuctoo," and Tennyson, apparently unwilling to devote much thought or labour to the task, sent home for this early poem on the somewhat incongruous theme of "Armageddon," which he adapted to the subject in hand. The poem won the prize, in spite of the fact that it was in blank verse instead of the rhyming couplet, which was still regarded as the only fitting metre for a prize poem, and in spite of an obscurity and lack of form which was no doubt partly due to the method of its composition.

 "Armageddon" is evidently very early work and this is probably an early draft, seeming from the handwriting to have been written when the poet was not more than fifteen. "Timbuctoo" was published in the Oxford University Press "Tennyson," edited by Sir T. Herbert Warren, and a comparison of the two poems shows that only a very small quantity of "Armageddon" was actually incorporated in "Timbuctoo," though there is a similarity between the general framework of the poems. In each an angel comes down to the poet when standing on a mountain.

"Timbuctoo" commences with the line—

"I stood upon the mountain which o'erlooks," which begins the second and third paragraphs of "Armageddon," though in the former poem the mountain overlooks not Megiddo but the Straits of Gibraltar. Then follow sixty lines in which the poet dreams of the legend of lost Atlantis, and asks if Africa still holds a city;

> "as fair
> As those which starr'd the night o' the Elder World?
> Or is the rumour of thy Timbuctoo
> A dream as frail as those of ancient times?"

Then comes the next similarity (cf. the opening lines of Part II of "Armageddon"):

> "A curve of whitening, flashing, ebbing light!
> A rustling of white wings! The bright descent
> Of a young seraph! And he stood beside me
> There on the ridge, and look'd into my face
> With his unutterable, shining orbs."

The seraph is then described in lines which do not occur in the earlier poem and asks the poet why he muses on these old legends and bids him open his eyes and see. Then follow the twenty-four lines from Armageddon which begin:

> "I look'd, but not upon his face,"

and end:

> "Beat like a far wave on my anxious ear,"

which are perhaps the best lines in both poems, and of interest as being a very early description by the poet of the mystical experience of separation of spirit from body, which he believed that he experienced from time to time (cf. "The Ancient Sage" and the early poem "The Mystic" quoted in the notes on that poem in the collected edition).

In "Timbuctoo" Tennyson inserted six new lines after

> "of her black hollows."

in the twenty-first line, and omitted the next fifteen lines of this fine passage, the only remaining similarity to "Armageddon" being the subsequent incorporation in quite a different context of the last six lines of Part II.

THE COACH OF DEATH[1]

(A fragment)

FAR off in the dun, dark Occident,
   Behind the burning Sun:
Where his gilding ray is never sent,
   And his hot steeds never run:

There lies a land of chilling storms,
   A region void of light,
A land of thin faces and shadowy forms,
   Of vapors, and mist, and night.

There never green thing will gaily spring
   In that unwholesome air,
But the rickety blast runs shrilly and fast
   Thro' the bony branches there.

When the shadow of night's eternal wings
   Envelopes the gloomy whole,
And the mutter of deep-mouth'd thunderings
   Shakes all the starless pole,

Thick sobs and short shrill screams arise
   Along the sunless waste,
And the things of past days with their horrible eyes
   Look out from the cloudy vast.

[1] Published by Hallam Lord Tennyson in his Memoir (see p. 23, one-volume edn.), and stated to have been written by the poet at fourteen or fifteen years of age (*ib.* p. 19).

And the earth is dry, tho' the pall of the sky
   Leave never an inch of blue;
And the moaning wind before it drives
   Thick wreaths of cloudy dew.

Whoever walks that bitter ground
   His limbs beneath him fail;
His heart throbs thick, his brain reels sick:
   His brow is clammy and pale.

But some have hearts that in them burn
   With power and promise high,
To draw strange comfort from the earth,
   Strange beauties from the sky.

Dark was the night, and loud the roar
   Of wind and mingled shower,
When there stood a dark coach at an old Inn door
   At the solemn midnight hour.

That Inn was built at the birth of Time:
   The walls of lava rose,
Cemented with the burning slime
   Which from Asphaltus flows.

No sound of joy, no revelling tones
   Of carouse were heard within:
But the rusty sign of a skull and cross-bones
   Swung creaking before the Inn.

No taper's light look'd out on the night,
   But ever and anon

Strange fiery eyes glared fiercely thro'
   The windows of shaven bone.

And the host came forth, and stood alone
   And still in the dark doorway:
There was not a tinge on each high cheek bone
   But his face was a yellow gray.

The skin hung lax on his long thin hands;
   No jolly host was he;
For his shanks were shrunken to willow wands
   And his name was Atrophy!

Dimly the travellers look'd thro' the glooms,
   Worn and wan was their gaze, I trow,
As the shrivell'd forms of the shadowy grooms
   Yoked the skeleton horses to.

They lifted their eyes to the dead, pale skies,
   And above the barkless trees
They saw the green verge of the pleasant earth,
   And heard the roar of her seas.

They see the light of their blest firesides,
   They hear each household voice:
The whisper'd love of the fair young wives;
   And the laugh of their rose-lipp'd boys.

The summer plains with their shining leaves,
   The summer hills they see;
The dark vine leaves round the rustling eaves,
   And the forests, fair and free.

There came a gaunt man from the dark Inn door,
    A dreadnought coat had he:
His bones crack'd loud, as he stept thro' the crowd,
    And his boots creak'd heavily.

Before his eyes so grim and calm
    The tingling blood grew chill,
As each put a farthing into his palm,
    To drive them where he will.

His sockets were eyeless, but in them slept
    A red infernal glow;
As the cockroach crept, and the white fly leapt
    About his hairless brow.

They mounted slow in their long black cloaks,
    The tears bedimm'd their sight;
The grim old coachee strode to the box,
    And the guard gasp'd out "All's right."

The leaders bounded, the guard's horn sounded:
    Far away thro' the night ran the lengthen'd tones:
As the quick wheels brush'd, and threw up the dust
    Of dead men's pulverised bones.

Whose blood in its liveliest course would not pause
    At the strife of the shadowy wheels,
The chattering of the fleshless jaws,
    And the beat of the horny heels?

Deep dells of snow sunk on each side below
    The highway, broad and flat,

As the coach ran on, and the sallow lights shone
   Dimly and blurly with simmering fat.

Vast wastes of starless glooms were spread
   Around in the chilling air,
And heads without bodies and shapes without heads
   Went leaping here and there.

O Coachee, Coachee, what lights approach
   With heavenly melodies?
Oh! those are the lights of the Paradise coach,
   That so gaily meet their eyes!

With pleasant hymns they soothe the air
   Of death, with songs of pride:
With sackbut, and with dulcimer,
   With psaltery they ride.

These fear not the mists of unwholesome damps
   That through that region rove,
For all wreath'd with green bays were the gorgeous
     lamps,
   And a bright archangel drove.

They pass'd (an inner spirit fed
   Their ever-burning fires,)
With a solemn burst of thrilling light,
   And a sound of stringéd lyres.

With a silver sound the wheels went round,
   The wheels of burning flame;
Of beryl, and of amethyst
   Was the spiritual frame.

Their steeds were strong exceedingly:
  And rich was their attire:
Before them flow'd a fiery stream;
  They broke the ground with hoofs of fire.

They glitter'd with a stedfast light,
  The happy spirits within;
As stars they shone, in raiment white,
  And free from taint of sin.

ODE: O BOSKY BROOK

O BOSKY brook, which I have lov'd to trace
Thro' all thy green and winding ways,
Wandering in the pure light of youthful days
    Along yon dusky windy hills,
Whose dark indent and wild variety
Curtails the Southern sky,
Following, thro' many a windy grove of pines,
White undergrowth of hemlock and hoar lines
Of sallows, whitening to the fitful breeze,
    The voiceful influx of thy tangled rills—
How happy were the fresh and dewy years
    When by thy damp and rushy side,
    In the deep yellow Eventide,
I wept sweet tears,
Watching the red hour of the dying Sun,
And felt my mind dilate
With solemn uncontrollable pleasure, when
The sad curve of the hueless Moon,
Sole in her state,
Varied with steadfast shades the glimmering plain,
And full of lovely light
Appear'd the mountain tarn's unbroken sleep,
Which never felt the dewy sweep
Of oars, but blackly lay
Beneath the sunny living noon,
Most like an insulated part of night,
Tho' fair by night as day:

So deep, that when day's manhood wears his crown
Of hottest rays in Heaven's windy Hall,
To one who pryeth curiously down,
From underneath the infathomable pall
    And pressure of the upright wave,
The abiding eyes of Space, from forth the grave
    Of that black Element,
Shine out like wonderful gleams
    Of thrilling and mysterious beauty, sent
From gay shapes sparkling thro' the gloom of dreams.

II

Well have I known thee, whatsoe'er thy phase,
In every time and place,
Pale Priestess of grey Night,
Whether thy flood of mournful rays,
Parted by dewless point of conic hill,
Adown its richer side
    Fell straying
Into the varied valley underneath;
Or where, within the eddying tide
Of some tumultuous mountain rill,
Like some delusive charm
Thy mimic form,
Full opposite to thy reality,
    Broken and flashing and playing
In tremulous darts of slender light,
Beguiled the sight;
Or on the screaming waste of desolate heath
In midnight full of sound,

Or in close pastures soft as dewy sleep,
Or in the hollow deep
Of woods, whose counterchang'd embroidery
Of light and darkness chequered the old moss
On the damp ground;
Or whether thou becamest the bright boss
    Of thine own Halo's dusky shield,[1]
        Or when thou burnest beaconlike upon
      The margin of the dun and dappled field
          Of vagrant waves, or higher ris'n, dost link
          Thy reflex to the steadfast brink,
With such a lustrous chord of solemn sheen,
That the heart vibrates with desire to pace
The palpitating track of buoyant rays;
    Or when the loud sea gambols and the spray
Of its confliction shoots and spreads and falls,
Blossoming round the everduring walls
        Which build up the giant cape,
          Whose mass'd and wonder-stirring shape
          And jutting head,
[2] Citadel-crowned and tempest-buffeted,
Runs far away,
(What time the white West glows with sickening ray)
And in the middle ocean meets the surging shock,
And plumes with snowy sheen each gather'd crest,
The lighthouse glowing from the secret rock,
The seabird piping on the wild salt waste.

  [1] Cf. Stanza IV of "The Voyage," published in 1864.
  [2] The line "Tempest-buffeted, citadel-crowned" occurs in the poem "Will" published in 1855.

III

I savour of the Egyptian and adore
Thee, venerable dark! august obscure!
    Sublimest Athor!
  It is not that I doat upon
    Thy glooms, because the weary mind is
      fraught
With fond comparison
Of thy deep shadow to its inward strife,
    But rather,
    That as thou wert the parent of all life,
E'en so thou art the mother of all thought,
Which wells not freely from the mind's recess
  When the sharp sunlight occupies the sense
With this fair world's exceeding comeliness,
    The goodly show and varied excellence
  Of lithe tall trees, the languor of sweet flowers
    Into the universal herbage woven,
      High hills and broad fair vallies river-cloven,
  Part strown with lordly cities and with towers,
Part spotted with the gliding white of pregnant sails;
Add murmur, which the buxom gales
    (As my glowing brows they fan)
      Bear upward thro' the happy heights
        of air,
      Chirp, bellow, bark and distant shout of
        man—
      Not that the mind is edged,
      Not that the spirit of thought is freshlier
        fledged

With stillness like the stillness of the tomb
And grossest gloom,
As it were of the inner sepulchre.
Rare sound, spare light will best address
The soul for awful muse and solemn watchfulness....

Note.—This fragment is evidently of early origin. A preliminary and less complete version exists in a notebook which contains some very early verses, apparently of about the date of "The Devil and the Lady" (written *aetat.* fourteen). The fragment is in three somewhat disconnected parts. The first is addressed to a brook, not the famous Holywell brook, though no doubt the description is, in parts, reminiscent of it, but to an imaginary mountain stream. The second is addressed to the moon, the last to darkness.

THE OUTCAST

I W I L L not seek my father's groves,
They murmur deeply o'er my head
Of sunless days and broken loves:
Their shade is dim and dark and dead.
There thro' the length of cool arcades,
Where noonday leaves the midnight dews,
Unreal shapes of twilight shades
Along the sombre avenues,
To Memory's widowed eyes would spring
In dreamy, drowsy wandering.

I will not seek my father's hills,
Their hue is fresh and clear and bright,
What time the early sunbeam fills
Their bush-clad depths with lonely light.
Each broken stile, each wavy path,
Each hollowed hawthorn, damp and black,
Each brook that chatters noisy wrath
Among its knotted reeds, bring back
Lone images of varied pain
To this worn mind and fevered brain.

I will not seek my father's hall:
There peers the day's unhallow'd glare,
The wet moss crusts the parting wall,
The wassail wind is reveller there.
Along the weedy, chinky floors

Wild knots of flowering rushes blow
And through the sounding corridors
The sere leaf rustles to and fro:
And oh! what memory might recall
If once I paced that voiceless Hall!

Note.—The MS. (not in Tennyson's hand) is initialled "A.T. 1826." The lines, therefore, date from the poet's seventeenth year.

IN DEEP AND SOLEMN DREAMS

I N deep and solemn dreams I view
Great cities by an ocean blue,
Terrace upon terrace bright
Standing out in sunny light,

And sheeny spires and turrets mixt
With pomp of burnish'd domes betwixt,
And pinnacles, and airy halls
With fairy fretwork on the walls,

And rows of pillars high and light,
That end in lines of streaky white,
Brooded o'er by dovelike rest,
Like a City of the Blest.

All adown the busy ways
Come sunny faces of lost days,
Long to mouldering dust consign'd,
Forms which live but in the mind.

Then methinks they stop and stand,
And I take each by the hand,
And we speak as we have spoken
Ere our love by death was broken.

With tearless ageless eyes that glisten
In light and tranquil mirth, they listen,
And as sleep the brain beguiles
Smile their old familiar smiles.

But ere long that silent sea,
Rising wild and wrathfully,
Sweeps in all-embracing might
Friends and city from my sight—
Then I lie and toss and mourn
Hopeless, heartless and forlorn.

Then I dream again, and lo!
Round me press a laughing row,
A careless, free and happy crowd,
With merry hearts and voices loud,
On the level sungirt lawn
Ere the glorious sun be born.

And I gaze without a tear
On their countenances clear,
On their noble foreheads white,
And their eyes divine with light—

"Hark away! 'tis early morn,
The East is crimson to the dawn,
We have waked the matin bird
And the brooks may yet be heard.

Brothers, come! the twilight's tears
Are heavy on the barley spears,
And the sweet winds tremble o'er
The large leaves of the sycamore.[1]

---

[1] Cf.   IN MEMORIAM XCV.
And sucked from out the distant gloom
  A breeze began to tremble o'er
    The large leaves of the sycamore,
And fluctuate all the still perfume,

Hark away! we'll weave to-day
A garland of all flowers gay,
Where the freshest flowers be
To the far wood walks will we."

Yet a little, brothers, keep
The sacred charm of tearless sleep—
Oh unkind! what darkening change
Hath made your features dim and strange!

Dear lips, loved eyes, ye fade, ye fly,
Even in my fear ye die,
And the hollow dark I dread
Closes round my friendless head,

And far away, to left and right,
Whirlwinds waste the dizzy night,
And I lie and toss and mourn,
Hopeless, heartless and forlorn.

Note.—There are several extant versions of this poem, which seems to have been begun at Somersby and finished at Cambridge.

MEMORY

A y me! those childish lispings roll
As thunder thro' my heart and soul,
Those fair eyes in my inmost frame
Are subtle shafts of pierceant flame.

Blesséd, curséd, Memory,
Shadow, Spirit as thou may'st be,
Why hast thou become to me
A conscience dropping tears of fire
On the heart, which vain desire
Vexeth all too bitterly?
When the wand of circumstance
All at once hath bid thee glance,
From the body of the Past,
Like a wandering ghost aghast,
Why wearest thou, mad Memory,
Lip and lip and hair and eye,[1]
Life—life without life or breath,
Death forth issuing from Death?

May goes not before dark December,
Nor doth the year change suddenly;
Wherefore do I so remember
That Hope is born of Memory
Nightly in the house of dreams?
But when I wake, at once she seems

[1] The first word of this line is very hard to decipher and I cannot guarantee the text.

The faery changeling wan Despair,
Who laughs all day and never speaks—
O dark of bright! O foul of fair!
A frightful child with shrivelled cheeks.

Why at break of cheerful day
Doth my spirit faint away
Like a wanderer in the night?
Why in visions of the night
Am I shaken with delight
Like a lark at dawn of day?
As a hungry serpent coiled
Round a palm tree in the wild,
When his bakéd jaws are bare
Burning in the burning air,
And his corky tongue is black
With the raging famine-crack,
If perchance afar he sees
Winding up among the trees,
Lordly-headed buffaloes,
Or but hears their distant lows,
With the fierce remembrance drunk
He crushes all the stalwart trunk
Round which his fainting folds are prest,
With delirium-causing throes
Of anticipated zest.

Note.—This fragment, which is very hastily written, occurs in the same notebook as the two preceding poems, "O Bosky Brook" and "In Deep and Solemn Dreams." It, too, appears to belong to the Somersby–Cambridge transition period.

PERDIDI DIEM

A N D thou hast lost a day! Oh mighty boast!
Dost thou miss one day only? I have lost
A life, perchance an immortality;
I never *liv'd* a day, but daily die,
    I have no real breath;
My being is a vacant worthlessness,
A carcase in the coffin of this flesh,
    Pierc'd thro' with loathly worms of utter Death.
My soul is but th' eternal mystic lamp,
Lighting that charnel damp,
Wounding with dreadful days that solid gloom,
And shadowing forth th' unutterable tomb,
Making a 'darkness visible'
Of that which without thee we had not felt
As darkness, dark ourselves and loving night,
Night-bats into the filtering crevices
Hook'd, clinging, darkness-fed, at ease:
Night-owls whose organs were not made for light.
I must needs pore upon the mysteries
Of my own infinite Nature and torment
My Spirit with a fruitless discontent:
As in the malignant light
Of a dim, dripping, moon-enfolding night,
Young ravens fallen from their cherishing nest
On the elm-summit, flutter in agony
With a continual cry
About its roots, and fluttering trail and spoil

PART II
CAMBRIDGE

SENSE AND CONSCIENCE

WORKING high Treason toward thy sovranty,
A traitorous and unfaithful minister,
Have I been lavish of thy treasures, Time.
Thy stores were shallow enow, but on their briefness
Have I drawn largely and often, hoping they
Were deeper than I found them, ill-informed,
An ignorant vain steward: they lie so thin now
I cannot choose but see their shallowness.
When they are wasted I am out of place,
And that must needs come quickly: for I have not
(As the condition of mine office ran)
Used them to furnish necessary wars
With fitting front of opposition,
And subtil temperament of harden'd arms,
Wherewith to embattail *Spirit*, whose fair ranks,
Strong in their essence but undisciplin'd,
Were shock'd and riv'n and shaken asunder wide,
And ridden over by the exulting *Sense*,
Their clamorous shrieks dust-stifled—
                              Rather, Time,
Unto the abuse of thy most precious ore,
Did I win over the Arch-Enemy *Sense*,
And set him in the chiefest offices
And heights of the State, unto the infinite rack
Of those few faithful in the land, which still
Cried out against my stewardship. Then Sense
Grew large and prosper'd at the court of Time,

Say rather, took away all thought of Time
By his own imminent greatness, and then first
Made me his bondsman, and by violence
Wrench'd from my grasp the golden keys which guard
The doors o' the Treasure-house. Great Conscience
    then,
The boldest of the warriors of Time,
Prime mover of those wars of Spirit and Sense,
The wisest of the councillors of Time,
Ere while my bosom friend, whose voice till now
Was loudest in the Council-room against
The prevalent Ministry, was drugg'd to sleep
By a most stealthy potion given by Sense—
To *sleep!* for neither edge of finest steel
Nor barbéd fire of spears, nor deadliest draught
Could drive him to the death: such subtlety
Of revivescence in his spirit lay,
Infus'd by his immortal Parentage,
Reason and Will!
               They drove him to deep shades,
A gloom monotonously musical
With hum of murmurous bees, which brooded deep
In ever-trembling flowers, and constant moan
Of waterfalls i' th' distance, and low winds
Wandering close to Earth, and voice of doves,
Which ever bowing cooed and cooing bowed
Unto each other as they could not cease.
Long time he lay and slept: his awful brows
Pillow'd on violet-woven mosses deep;
The irrepressible power of his keen eyes
Burn'd thro' the shadow of their down-dropt lids;
One hand was flung to distance; the barr'd iron

Of battle-writhen sinews crush'd and mass'd
The pleasurable flowers; the other grasp'd
The hilt of that great blade of puissant flame
Hight the *heart-cleaver*.
                      Alway in his sight
Delicious dreams floated unto the music
Of winds (whose fragrance and whose melodies
Made sweet contention which should sweeter be,
And thro' contention grew to perfectness
Of most inviolate communion),
And witching fantasies which won the heart,
Lovely with bright black eyes and long black hair
And lips which moved in silence, shaping words
With meaning all too sweet for sound.
                                  At last
Came Memory wandering from afar, with stern
Sad eyes and temples wan cinctur'd with yew;
Pain went before her alway half turn'd round
To meet her coming with drawn brows low-bent
Whetting a dart on which her tears fell ever,
Softening the stone that she might point the steel.
The Giant rais'd his eyes and saw and knew
The blackness of her shadow where she stood
Between him and the moonlight of his soul.
He started to his feet, but lacking strength
From so long sleep fell prone, and tears of fire
Wept, filling all the joyous flower-cups
With burning blight and odour-quenching sighs,
So that their golden colours fell away
O'er-flown with pale. Rage seiz'd upon him then
And grasping with both palms his wondrous blade,
Sheer through the summit of the tallest flowers

He drave it: the rose fell, the argent lily,
The dappled fox-glove with its poison'd leaves,
And the tall poppy fell, whose eminent flower,
Hued with the crimson of a fierce sunrise,
Like to the wild youth of an evil King
Is without sweetness, but who crowns himself
Above the secret poisons of his heart
In his old age. The ivy from the stem
Was torn, the vine made desolate; his feet
Were crimson'd with its blood, from which flows joy
And bitterness, first joy from bitterness,
And then again great bitterness from joy.
Soon shrouding with his hand his guilty eyes,
Into the heart of the realm afar he fled
And lived on little roots which memory
Dug for him round his cell.
       One solemn night
He could not sleep, but on the bed of thorns,
Which Memory and Pain had strown for him,
Of brambles and wild thistles of the wood,
Lay tossing, hating light and loathing dark,
And in his agony his heart did seem
To send up to his eyes great drops of blood,
Which would not fall because his burning eyes
Did hiss them into drought. Aloud he wept,
Loud did he weep, for now the iron had come
Into his soul: the hollow vaulted caverns
Bore out his heavy sobs to the waste night,
And some the low-browed arch return'd unto
His ear; so sigh from sigh unceasing grew. . . .

 Note.—These lines are an unfinished allegory of the struggle between Sense and Conscience. The giant whose fate is here described is Conscience; he is drugged by the adherents of Sense and cast out into a remote forest. The poem is contained in a notebook inscribed: "A. Tennyson, Trin: Coll:, Cambridge." The poppy simile was afterwards transplanted to "The Lover's Tale." I have omitted one very involved and obviously imperfect passage of ten lines, the deletion of which causes no interruption of the sense.

"ILION, ILION"

ILION, Ilion, dreamy Ilion, pillared Ilion, holy Ilion,
City of Ilion when wilt thou be melody born?
Blue Scamander, yellowing Simois from the heart of
    piny Ida
Everwhirling from the molten snows upon the
    mountainthrone,
Roll Scamander, ripple Simois, ever onward to a
    melody
Manycircled, overflowing thoro' and thoro' the
    flowery level of unbuilt Ilion,
City of Ilion, pillared Ilion, shadowy Ilion, holy Ilion,
    To a music merrily flowing, merrily echoing
    When wilt thou be melody born?

Manygated, heavywalléd, manytowered city of Ilion,
From the silver, lilyflowering meadowlevel
    When wilt thou be melody born?
Ripple onward, echoing Simois,
Ripple ever with a melancholy moaning,
    In the rushes to the dark blue brimméd Ocean,
    yellowing Simois,
To a music from the golden twanging harpwire
    heavily drawn.
    Manygated, heavywalléd, manytowered city of
    Ilion,
    To a music sadly flowing, slowly falling,
    When wilt thou be melody born?

MARION

T H O U art not handsome, no, nor plain,
  And thou dost own no graceful art,
Thou hast no little winning ways
Whereby to win our love or praise,
    Yet holdest thou an ample reign
      Within the human heart.
It is a sort of pride in thee,
    In every shade of joy or woe
    Still with the general mood to flow,
    Nor more nor less, but ever so.
What is it oversteps this law,
And overshowers the daily and the real
    As with a fruitful rain of grace?
    Let me die, Marion, if I ever saw
    Such ideal unideal,
      Such uncommon commonplace!
Though thought and art and speech in thee
  Run parallel with thought and speech
In the universal Mind,
    My gentle Marion, couldst thou teach
      That peculiar alchemy
  To the rest of womankind,
Which evermore to precious ore
    Changes common thought in thee,
    That spiritual economy,
Which wasteth not itself in signs,
And yet with power intertwines
    Thine image with the memory,

The world would build thee silver shrines.
   From what far inward source
     Is that rare influence drawn,
   Enlightening all intercourse
   With thee, my quiet Marion?
Which can illustrate every nameless act,
   And from the eyelids of hardfeatured fact
   Rain tender starlight on the heart?
   That magically woven net
     Thou threwest round me when we met,
      Thin-threaded as the cobweb round
   In a corner of the glass,
     Wherewith the green-winged moth is bound
     And seeth not and cannot pass.
It is the slow-increased delight
   Of unperceivéd gentleness,
That touching with scarce visible ray
The barren light of every day,
   Possesseth all its nakedness
With stealing shadows dusk and bright.

Love is a vine, and in the hot
   And southern slopes he takes delight;
   He curls his tendrils in thy light,
But his grape clusters ripen not:
But mild affection taketh root
   And prospers in thy placid light.
Thou art the soul of commonplace
   The body all mankind divide.—

Note.—A note in the handwriting of Hallam Lord Tennyson attributes this poem to the Cambridge period. The last two lines do not fit into the rhyme scheme, so "Marion" cannot be regarded as a finished work.

AMY

HIGHMINDED and pure-thoughted, chaste and
    simple,
  In Life's broad river set
A lily, where the waters faintly dimple,
  Leaving the flower unwet;
The silver tongues of featherfooted rumour
  Ne'er spake of thee to me,
Thou hast no range of wit, no wealth of humour,
  But pure humility
Dwelling like moonlight in a silver vapour;
  Not pale St. Agatha
Bent o'er her missal by her waxen taper,
  Not sweet Cecilia,
St. Agnes on St. Agnes' Eve, who leadeth
  Over the snowy hill
Her snowwhite lambs and with hushed footstep
    treadeth,
  Is not so chaste and still
In the cold moon, e'er yet the crocus flamy
  Or snowdrop burst to life;
Yet with a human love I love thee, Amy,
  And woo thee for my wife. . . .
Dear sainted Amy, thou dost never tremble
  To starts or thrills of love,
But rather in thy motion dost resemble
  Hill-shaded streams, that move
Through the umber glebe and in brown deeps embosom
  The tremulous Evenstar,

Fold within fold thou growest, a virgin blossom,
   In dewy glades afar . . .
Yet take blind Passion; give him eyes; and freeing
   His spirit from his frame
Make double-natured love lose half his being
   In thy spiritual flame,
Till like a rainbow in a rainbow folded
   And of a rainbow made,
My spirit within thy spirit may be moulded,
   My soul of thine the shade.

Note.—These lines are from the same pocket-book as the "Ilion" fragment in what is apparently a hurried first draft of a poem which the poet intended to revise. Some lines are very hard to decipher and I have omitted two passages, which were obviously very imperfect. So much is necessary to explain the poem's evident defects, in spite of which I think it has qualities which justify its publication.

SONNET

S H E took the dappled partridge fleckt with blood,
    And in her hand the drooping pheasant bare,
    And by his feet she held the woolly hare,
And like a master-painting where she stood,
Lookt some new goddess of an English wood.
    Nor could I find an imperfection there,
    Nor blame the wanton act that showed so fair—
To me whatever freak she plays is good.
Hers is the fairest Life that breathes with breath,
    And *their* still plumes and azure eyelids closed
    Made quiet Death so beautiful to see
That Death lent grace to Life and Life to Death
    And in one image Life and Death reposed,
    To make my love an Immortality.

SONNET

ALAS! how weary are my human eyes
   With all the thousand tears of human scorn.
   Alas! how like the dappled moon at morn
My waning spirit after darkness sighs.
Thro' kindling buds hale March will yearly blow
   On hollow winds his gusty showerdrops,
   And many an April sprinkle the blue copse
With snowy sloethorn-flowers when I am low,
And brown September laughing cheerily
   Bruise his gold grain upon his threshing-floor,
And all the infinite variety
   Of the dear world will vary evermore.
     Close weary eyes, breathe out my weary breath,
     One only thought I have, and that is death.

SONNET

W o e to the double-tongued, the land's disease,
   Lords of the hustings, whose mob-rhetoric rends
   The ears of Truth! How shall they make amends,
Those that would shatter England's ancient ease
Built on broad bases and the solid peace
   Wherein she prospered?—Woe to those false friends
   That mouth great things and for their own vile ends
Make swarm with brazen clang the humming bees;
   Those that would turn the ploughshares into swords,
   Those that inflame themselves with idle words
In every market-place. Their doom is signed,
   Tho' they shall cause confusion and the storms
   Of civil blood—Moths, cankers, palmer-worms
That gnaw the bud, blind leaders of the blind.

SONNET

Ah, fade not yet from out the green arcades,
    Fade not, sweet Rose, for hark! the woodland shrills,
A lamentation grows in all the shades,
    And grief in copses where the linnet trills:
    The sweet Rose fades from all the winding rills
And waning arches of the golden glades:
    From all the circuit of the purple hills
The sweet Rose fades, alas, how soon it fades.
It does not fade, but from the land it goes,
    And leaves the land to winter. I remain,
    To waste alone the slowly-narrowing days.
It fades to me: for they transplant the Rose,
    And further South the Rose will bloom again
    Like a mere Rose that only cares for praise.

Note.—The last line suggests that the lament is for the departure of some human rose from the Somersby district.

SONNET

I LINGERED yet awhile to bend my way
   To that far South, for which my spirits ache,
For under rainy hills a jewel lay
   And this dark land was precious for its sake,
   A rosy-coloured jewel, fit to make
An emperor's signet-ring, to save or slay
   Whole peoples, such as some great King might take
To clasp his mantle on a festal day:
And yet a jewel only made to shine,
   And icy cold although 'tis rosy clear—
     Why did I linger? I myself condemn,
For ah! 'tis far too costly to be mine,
   And nature never dropt a human tear
     In those chill dews whereof she froze the gem.

Note.—Tennyson in his youth had a great longing to go and live in some Mediterranean country, as his eldest brother, Frederick, did soon after leaving Cambridge. The sonnet is rather obscure, but I think the "Jewel" was human and feminine.

SONNET

WHEN that rank heat of evil's tropic day
   Made floating cloud of flowing joy, and cleft
My shores of life (their freshness steamed away,
   Nothing but salt and bitter crystals left),
When in my lonely walks I seemed to be
   An image of the cursed figtree, set
   In the brown glens of this Mount Olivet,
Thy looks, thy words, were sun and rain to me.
When all sin-sickened, loathing my disgrace,
   Far on within the temple of the mind
      I seemed to hear God speaking audibly,
"Let us go hence"—sometimes a little space,
   Out of the sphere of God, I dared to find
      A shadow and a resting place in thee.

Note.—This sonnet expresses a characteristic mood of depression and self-depreciation. Possibly the friend to whom it was addressed was Arthur Hallam.

SONNET

CONRAD! why call thy life monotonous?
   Why brood above thine anchor? the wov'n weed
   Calms not, but blackens, the slope water bed.
The shores of Life are fair and various,
   But thou dost ever by one beach abide.
Why hast thou drawn thine oars across the boat?
Thou canst not without impulse downward float,
   The wave of life hath no propelling tide.
We live but by *resistance*, and the best
   Of Life is but the struggle of the will:
   Thine unresisting boat shall pause—not still
But beaten on both sides by swaying Unrest.
Oh! cleave this calm to living eddies, breast
   This sloth-sprung weed with progress sensible.

MILTON'S MULBERRY

L o o k what love the puddle-pated squarecaps have
    for me!
I am Milton's mulberry, Milton's Milton's mulberry—
But they whip't and rusticated him who planted me,
Milton's Milton's mulberry, Milton's Milton's mul-
    berry.
Old and hollow, somewhat crooked in the shoulders as
    you see,
Full of summer foliage yet but propt and padded
    curiously,
I would sooner have been planted by the hand that
    planted me,
Than have grown in Paradise and dropped my fruit on
    Adam's knee—
Look what love the tiny-witted Trenchers have for me.

Note.—This poem, which is clearly of the Cambridge period, refers, of course, to the mulberry tree at Christ's College, reported to have been planted by the poet.

THE RUINED KILN

I

A MILLION gossamers in field and fold
Were twinkling into green and gold,
Then basked the filmy stubbles warm and bare,
While thousands in a silent air
   Of dappled cloudlets roofed the day,
And sparrows in a jangling throng
Chirped all in one—a storm of song—
   As by the ruined kiln I lay.

II

All else like me, one peaceful presence kept,
On his bound sheaf October slept,
Thro' crumbling bricks the woolly thistle grew;
Yet in the round kiln slept the dew
   And, over harrowed glebe, was seen
Hard by one waning elm, the farm,
In tempered sunshine white and warm,
   Where Lucy lived the village-queen.

Note.—These lines occur in a small pocket-book, which is dated in Hallam Tennyson's handwriting 1831–33, and I have found a slightly different version written by Tennyson in ink in a proof copy of the volume of 1832.

which the stanzas are printed is in the handwriting of Emily Lady Tennyson, and evidently of a much later date. It is interesting to note that some other stanzas of the long poem were used, with slight adaptations, in "In Memoriam" (published 1850), the "Ode on the Death of the Duke of Wellington" (1852) and "Lines to the Marquis of Dufferin and Ava" (1889), forming in each case some of the most effective lines in the poem concerned.

(WHAT THOR SAID TO THE BARD BEFORE DINNER)

  WHEREVER evil customs thicken
Break thro' with the hammer of iron rhyme,
 Till priest-craft and king-craft sicken,
But pap-meat-pamper not the time
 With the flock of the thunder-stricken.
If the world caterwaul, lay harder upon her
 Till she clapperclaw no longer,
 Bang thy stithy stronger and stronger,
Thy rhyme-hammer *shall* have honour.

  Be not fairspoken neither stammer,
Nail her, knuckle her, thou swinge-buckler!
 Spare not: ribroast gaffer and gammer,
Be no shuffler, wear no muffler,
 But on thine anvil hammer and hammer!
If she call out lay harder upon her,
  This way and that nail
  Tag rag and bobtail,
Thy rhyme-hammer *shall* have honour.

  On squire and parson, broker and banker,
Down let fall thine iron spanker,
 Spare not king or duke or critic,
Dealing out cross-buttock and flanker
 With thy clanging analytic!
If she call out lay harder upon her,

NEW YEAR'S EVE

Listen! bells in yonder town,
   Lin, lan, lone,
Over dale and over down,
   Lin, lan, lone,
Now the year is almost gone,
   Lin, lan, lone,
Dying, dying, almost gone,
   Lin, lan, lone,
Almost, almost, almost gone.

Listen how the bells begin,
   With a lin, lan, lin,
For the old year out and the new year in,
   With a lin-lan-lan and a lan-lan-lin,
And the old year out and the new year in,
   With a clash and a lin-lan-lin.

Put out the lights and let us go to bed,
The baby year is born, his father's dead,
And, settling back after that storm of sound,
From all the starry circle overhead
Hard silence drops upon the stony ground.

Note.—Cf. "The Mellow lin-lan-lone of Evening Bells" in "Far-Far-Away"—published 1889.

AN IDLE RHYME

Oh, what care I how many a fluke
   Sticks in the liver of the time?
I cannot prate against the Duke,
   I love to have an idle rhyme.

The muse would stumble from the tune,
   If I should ask her "Plump my purse,
Be for some popular forenoon
   The leading article in verse."

So gross a murmur in her ear
   Would make her dull as Davy's sow,
And with a sudden mildew sear
   The rathe fruitblossom on her brow.

For, though she has her hopes and fears,
   She dwells not on a single page,
But thrids the annals of the years,
   And runs her eye from age to age.

What's near is large to modern eyes,
   But disproportions fade away
Lower'd in the sleepy pits where lies
   The dropsied Epos of the day—

The day that rose like ours sublime
   In dreaming dreams and planning plans,
That thought herself the crown of time
   And took her many geese for swans.

Interfusa vadis, et quos fumantia torquens
Aequora vorticibus Phlegethon perlustrat anhelis;
Vos mihi sacrarum penetralia pandite rerum,
Et vestri secreta poli: qua lampade Ditem
Flexit Amor, quo ducta ferox Proserpina raptu
Possedit dotale Chaos, quantasque per oras
Sollicito genetrix erraverit anxia cursu:
Unde datae populis leges, et glande relicta
Cesserit inventis Dodonia quercus aristis.

   Dux Erebi quondam tumidas exarsit in iras
Proelia moturus Superis, quod solus egeret
Connubii, sterilesque diu consumeret annos,
Impatiens nescire torum, nullasque mariti
Illecebras, nec dulce patris cognoscere nomen.
Iam quaecunque latent ferali monstra barathro
In turmas aciemque ruunt, contraque Tonantem
Conjurant Furiae: crinitaque sontibus hydris
Tisiphone, quatiens infausto lumine pinum,
Armatos ad castra vocat pallentia Manes.
Paene reluctatis iterum pugnantia rebus
Rupissent elementa fidem, penitusque revulso
Carcere, laxatis pubes Titania vinclis
Vidisset caeleste jubar, rursusque cruentus
Aegaeon positis arcto de corpore nodis
Obvia centeno vexasset fulmina motu.
Sed Parcae vetuere minas, orbique timentes
Ante pedes soliumque ducis fudere severam
Canitiem, genibusque suas cum supplice vultu
Admovere manus, quarum sub jure tenentur
Omnia, quae seriem fatorum pollice ducunt,
Longaque ferratis evolvunt secula pensis.

   Prima fero Lachesis clamabat talia regi,

Incultas dispersa comas: O maxime noctis
Arbiter, umbrarumque potens, cui nostra laborant
Stamina, qui finem cunctis et semina praebes,
Nascendique vices alterna morte rependis:
Qui vitam letumque regis: (nam quicquid ubique
Gignit materies, hoc te donante creatur,
Debeturque tibi, certisque ambagibus aevi
Rursus corporeos animae mittuntur in ortus:)
Ne pete firmatas pacis dissolvere leges,
Quas dedimus, nevitque colus: neu foedera fratrum
Civili converte tuba.   Cur impia tollis
Signa? quid incestis aperis Titanibus auras?
Posce Iovem, dabitur conjux. Vix illa: pepercit,
Erubuitque preces, animisque relanguit atrox,
Quamvis indocilis flecti.   Ceu turbine rauco
Cum gravis armatur Boreas, glacieque nivali
Hispidus, et Getica concretus grandine pennas
Bella cupit, pelagus, silvas, camposque sonoro
Flamine rapturus: si forte adversus aenos
Aeolus objecit postes, vanescit inanis
Impetus, et fractae redeunt in claustra procellae.
   Tum Maia genitum, qui fervida dicta reportet,
Imperat acciri.   Cyllenius adstitit ales,
Somniferam quatiens virgam, tectusque galero.
Ipse rudi fultus solio, nigraque verendus
Majestate sedet: squalent immania foedo
Sceptra situ: sublime caput maestissima nubes
Asperat, et dirae riget inclementia formae.
Terrorem dolor augebat.   Tunc talia celso
Ore tonat: (tremefacta silent dicente tyranno
Atria: latratum triplicem compescuit ingens
Ianitor, et presso lacrymarum fonte resedit

Cocytos, tacitisque Acheron obmutuit undis,
Et Phlegethonteae requierunt murmura ripae:)
   Atlantis Tegaee nepos, commune profundis
Et superis numen, qui fas per numen utrumque
Solus habes, geminoque facis commercia mundo,
I celeres proscinde Notos, et jussa superbo
Redde Iovi. Tantumne tibi, saevissime fratrum,
In me juris erit?